MW01536121

Dealing with Defiance

by Charles R. Swindoll

ZondervanPublishingHouse

Grand Rapids, Michigan

A Division of HarperCollins*Publishers*

Dealing with Defiance: God's Plan for Overcoming Rebellion
© 1986, 1987, 1995 by Charles R. Swindoll, Inc.

Requests for information should be addressed to:
Zondervan Publishing House
5300 Patterson Avenue S.E.
Grand Rapids, Michigan 49530

ISBN 0-310-20074-1

Unless otherwise identified, all Scripture references are from the New American Standard Bible, © The Lockman Foundation 1960, 1962, 1963, 1968, 1971, 1972, 1973, 1975, 1977. Used by permission.

All rights reserved. No part of this publication may be reproduced, stored in a retrieval system, or transmitted in any form—electronic, mechanical, photocopy, recording, or any other—without the prior permission of the publisher.

Printed in the United States of America

Cover Design by DesignTeam, Brian L. Fowler

95 96 97 98 00 / ❖ DP / 5 4 3 2 1

Introduction

Foolishness is bound up in the heart of a
child;

The rod of discipline will remove it far
from him. (Prov. 22:15)

For rebellion is as the sin of divination, and
insubordination is as iniquity and idolatry. (1 Sam. 15:23a)

Good understanding produces favor, but
the way of the treacherous is hard.
(Proverbs 13:15)

I will instruct you and teach you in the way
which you should go;

I will counsel you with My eye upon you.

Do not be as the horse or as the mule. (Ps.
32:8–9a)

There were those who dwelt in darkness
and in the shadow of death,

Prisoners in misery and chains,

Because they had rebelled against the
words of God,

And spurned the counsel of the Most High.

Therefore He humbled their heart with
labor;

They stumbled and there was none to help.
(Ps. 107:10–12)

Now do not stiffen your neck like your
fathers, but yield to the Lord ... that His
burning anger may turn away from you.
(2 Chron. 30:8)

But realize this, that in the last days diffi-
cult times will come. For men will be
lovers of self, lovers of money, boastful,

arrogant, revilers, disobedient to parents, ungrateful, unholy. (2 Tim. 3:1–2)

Although the term *defiance* does not appear in Scripture, acts and attitudes of defiance often do. No matter what term is used, the scene is never pretty. The same is true in life today ... but the tragedy is that defiance is frequently permitted and sometimes totally ignored, leaving others in the wake of its serious consequences.

God never overlooks or winks at defiance. He deals with it, and we are to take our cues from our Lord. This booklet is about dealing with defiance—not only how God does it, but how we are to do it.

May He use these words to help you detect defiance and then strengthen your determination to deal with it.

Charles R. Swindoll

Dealing with Defiance

No one should be surprised that our days are marked by rebellion, stubbornness, arrogance, and defiance. These things were predicted to occur *"in the last days"* (2 Tim. 3:1–2), and they are right on schedule! The defiance may be as small and hidden as a toddler's temper tantrum or as hideous and treacherous as a terrorist attack in an airport. Whatever the case, defiance must be counteracted. To yawn and look the other way is *never* appropriate.

If people from another planet were to suddenly appear on Earth, I think they would be shocked. As they observed our lawless lifestyle, watched the proceedings of our divorce courts, read about crime on our streets, felt the pressure and anger from our homes, and listened to arguments in our school classrooms, they could get the idea that defiance pays off. It would appear that those who break the law and defy authority get away with it.

Homes are often dangerous places to be, permitting rebellion and intimidation. Children are in control. Parents have taken the passive route, giving their kids the authority. I don't know if you followed one particular case in Boulder, Colorado, but a young man sued his parents for parental malpractice, claiming $350,000 in damages. His complaint was that they had inflicted him with intentional emotional distress. At the time I read of it, the court apparently was falling back in favor of the parents' argument that it was not willful and wanton. They were hoping to win the case, but they weren't sure they would. When I was a little boy that case never would have made it to court. It would have been seen as contempt for authority instead of "child's rights."

Do you realize that your chance of becoming a victim of crime has doubled in just ten years? Your chance of becoming a victim of a *violent* crime has increased by more than five times in the same period. Today you have a one in twenty chance of being a victim of any crime. You have a one in one hundred chance of being a victim of a violent offense.

The scene isn't limited to a gang of local thugs. Defiance occurs in the national arena as well. When calamities occur across our land, it is amazing how many people gather, not to give aid, but to steal possessions from helpless victims of the tragedy. I find that shockingly unconscionable. Back in 1975, three tornadoes ripped through Omaha, Nebraska, destroying 500 homes, damaging 1,000 others, killing 3 people, and injuring over 130 residents. National Guardsmen were called out, not to help in the calamity, but to patrol a 3,400-square-block area to prevent looting. The Nebraska governor surveyed the area and said it was the worst case of property damage in the history of Nebraska. What a sad commentary on our modern society! Military men with weapons were needed to prevent scavengers from helping themselves to victims' belongings in the devastated sections of that Nebraska city.

A COMMENTARY ON DEFIANCE

The best commentary on humanity's defiance is not found in any book, television documentary, magazine, or newspaper. It is found in Scripture . . . God's book of truth. Specifically, in the last four verses of Romans 1. These verses peel off all masks, scrape away all the veneer, and get right down to the core of depravity, portraying mankind as

> being filled with all unrighteousness, wickedness, greed, evil; full of envy, murder, strife, deceit, malice; they are gossips, slanderers, haters of God, insolent, arrogant, boastful, inventors of evil,

disobedient to parents, without understanding, untrustworthy, unloving,
unmerciful; and, although they know the
ordinance of God, that those who practice such things are worthy of death, they
not only do the same, but also give
hearty approval to those who practice
them. (vv. 29–32)

Tough talk, huh? But true, painfully
true. And realistic. More honest than an arti-
cle out of *Time* or *Newsweek*, these verses pro-
vide us with an up-to-date commentary on
the extent of defiance today.

How does God deal with that kind of
stuff? What is His attitude toward rebellion
that is *that* blatant? How about when it
occurs in the lives of His children? It would
be wonderful if we could say that defiance is
limited to the life of the unbeliever, but that
simply is not the case. As a matter of fact,
some of you reading this booklet have to
confess that you wrestle with the problem of
defiance. That's why you started reading it.
Your rebellion has come out in your home. It
has begun to affect your work. Even your
relationships with people have been hin-
dered because of it. Perhaps your church
involvements have as well. Defiance, stubbornness, and rebellion rear their ugly heads
in every corner of life.

HOW GOD FEELS ABOUT DEFIANCE

How did God deal with defiance in biblical times? Before we examine the life of one whom God dealt with, let's take a quick look at His attitude, His abhorrence of rebellious acts. Please consider Deuteronomy 21:18–21. Even though this event occurred in the days when the severity of punishment was much greater than today, it nevertheless reveals how strongly the Lord feels about defiance.

I take it, from the way this narrative unfolds, that the person in question is a young man—old enough to live outside the home, but perhaps not quite ready for that. He's living under the roof of his parents, but he has been demonstrating insubordinate independence. His lifestyle reveals an unbending determination to have his own way.

> If any man has a stubborn and rebellious son who will not obey his father or his mother, and when they chastise him, he will not even listen to them, then his father and mother shall seize him, and bring him out to the elders of his city at the gateway of his home town. And they shall say to the elders of his city, "This son of ours is stubborn and rebellious, he will not obey us, he is a glutton and a drunkard." Then all the men of his city shall stone him to death; so you shall remove the evil from your midst, and all Israel shall hear of it and fear.

I remember the very first time I read that passage; I was a teenager! In fact, I was getting pretty big for my britches. I thought about those words till very late in the evening, believe me. I can still remember the chill that ran down my back when I realized how seriously God feels about defiance. I was also grateful that I was not living under the Law! The Lord made no provision for domestic insolence, even when the child living at home was approaching adulthood. Defiance is never excusable, never of little concern.

Before proceeding, perhaps I should clarify that this passage is not suggesting that parents have the right to be despotic dictators in the home, mistreating and manipulating their children. No! Please observe that the parents mentioned in Deuteronomy 21 apparently had attempted to work with their son—to no avail. He defied their authority. He refused to cooperate, to curtail his habit of getting drunk, to restrain himself in other things as well. This young man was turning the home into a "hell on earth." He left the parents with no alternative other than to call on city authorities to help, which still occurs today.

Take time to observe, parents! The peace, the moral standards, and the joy of your home are not to be sacrificed on the altar of indulgence. Defiance will ruin a home just as it will ruin a life. If you do not deal with it, who will? Believe me, the teacher at school or the minister at church cannot take the place of the parent at home.

In the days of Samuel, there once lived a king named Saul. He was terribly self-willed. On one occasion King Saul did his own thing. The prophet-judge Samuel was dispatched by the Lord to face the king. Saul excused himself, backpedaled, rationalized, and even denied being defiant. Finally, Samuel had had enough. He looked straight at Saul, pointed that long, bony finger of his and said, *"Rebellion is as the sin of divination . . . and idolatry."* That's quite a statement! The Living Bible captures the thought in this paraphase:

> For rebellion is as bad as the sin of witchcraft, and stubbornness is as bad as worshiping idols. (1 Sam. 15:23a)[1]

The next time you're tempted to pass over defiance, remember that analogy.

AN EXAMPLE OF HOW GOD DEALT WITH DEFIANCE

King Saul may have been rebellious . . . but King Solomon's story is even more incredible. Although bright, rich, capable, and from respectable roots, Solomon became an insolent, carnal man. We need to see how God dealt with him—the epitome of defiance.

The part of Solomon's biography that interests us is recorded in 1 Kings 11. This is not a teenaged, rebellious son living under the roof of his parents; this is a middle-aged man who has reached the pinnacle of success. (Remember, there is no age restriction on defiance—you can be defiant and be up in years. You can be defiant as a child, a teenager, or an adult.) By now Solomon was "running the show" of the kingdom. But, like a bolt out of the blue, he broke free. He must have thought, "I'm going to get my way regardless." He seemed to change overnight. And when that happens, it's time for people like us to sit up and learn some lessons. Solomon's life continues to be a warning to all of us.

SEEDS SOLOMON PLANTED

Actually, Solomon's defiance was not a sudden thing ... not at all. There were some seeds he had planted early in life which he later harvested in adulthood. The first were seeds of *compromise.* Remember when he had an alliance with Pharaoh, and he married Pharaoh's daughter? The story is recorded in 1 Kings, chapter 3. As a result of that compromising alliance, he began to make concessions in his spiritual walk. The compromise seeds grew into a loss of distinction as a sensitive man of God. He lost his distinction as a monotheistic Jewish ruler. He had been instructed not to cohabit or even mingle with foreign women. His Jewish upbringing included strong admonitions against intermarrying with Gentiles. The seeds of compromise were now harvested in a loss of distinction.

A little later on in his life, Solomon planted seeds of *extravagance.* Once they grew, they yielded boredom and cynicism, which is par for the course. He lived extravagantly. He spent extravagantly. He built extravagantly. There were no parameters on his budget. He was able to buy at will, build whatever he desired, and live wherever he wished. Self-control and restraint were not in his vocabulary. In the journal he kept, Ecclesiastes, we discover that his fast-lane, go-for-broke lifestyle led to cynicism, boredom, and disillusionment. Such is the fruit of extravagance.

Third, there was *unaccountability.* The more closely you study his managerial habits, the more you realize Solomon never was willing to be accountable—not to any of his counselors, not to any of the prophets, not to any of his wives who surrounded him. We never read of Solomon's asking for straight answers or listening to sound advice. He mentions the wisdom of it, theoretically, in the book of Proverbs, but it is conspicuously absent in his life. He operated like the Lone Ranger. He was closed-minded. Ultimately, he even ignored what God was saying through His spokesmen, which is lethal for any spiritual leader. The seeds of unaccountability were finally harvested. The fruit? Unchecked independence.

Nobody can get away with unaccountability. After a while you've got to pay the piper. And that's what Solomon did in the latter years of his life.

One more category of seeds should be mentioned—the seeds of *idolatry*. When harvested, idolatry led to lust and open defiance.

This is precisely where we find Solomon in 1 Kings 11. The man is living in the backwash of carnality. He doesn't know it, but he is about to be dealt with by the Lord God . . . who always takes a dim view of defiance.

> Now King Solomon loved many foreign women along with the daughter of Pharaoh: Moabite, Ammonite, Edomite, Sidonian, and Hittite women, from the nations concerning which the Lord had said to the sons of Israel, "You shall not associate with them, neither shall they associate with you, for they will surely turn your heart away after their gods." Solomon held fast to these in love.
> (vv. 1–2)

Solomon not only married foreign women, he married *many* of them, in direct defiance of Scripture. Defiance always denies Scripture willfully—not ignorantly, *willfully*.

And did you notice how verse 2 closes? *"Solomon held fast to these in love."* He flaunted his defiance. He not only embraced these women, he embraced them publicly. He not only married them, he courted them in front of the people of Israel. He not only played around ... he held fast to them in love.

We should not be surprised to read in the very next verse that *"his wives turned his heart away."* We don't use that expression today. We use the words "turned off." He was "turned off" to spiritual things. The Berkeley Bible says that those women *"perverted his mind."*[2] The foreign women, coming in with their idolatrous and cultural polytheism, brought with them enough seduction to turn him off spiritually. Solomon lived his final years turned off to God, which resulted in open defiance.

> For it came about when Solomon was old, his wives turned his heart away after other gods; and his heart was not wholly devoted to the Lord his God, as the heart of David his father had been. For Solomon went after Ashtoreth the goddess of the Sidonians and after Milcom the detestable idol of the Ammonites. And Solomon did what was evil in the sight of the Lord, and did not follow the Lord fully, as David his father had done. Then Solomon built a high place for Chemosh the detestable idol of Moab, on the mountain which is east of Jerusalem, and for Molech the detestable idol of the sons of Ammon. Thus also he did for all his foreign wives, who burned incense and sacrificed to their gods. (vv. 4–8)

Solomon's defiance was not hidden; it was out in the open.

Defiance is always a tough thing to deal with. If you have a defiant mate, it's a hard thing to live with. Some mates are so defiant it takes a harsh argument for the partner to bring to their attention the wrong in their lives. Some children and teens are so defiant that just mentioning their rebellion sets off an incredible explosion in the home. Pastors deal with defiance rather frequently. Sometimes it's a defiant board member . . . or church member . . . or fellow staff member. To be truthful, sometimes it's the pastor who has become a rebel—a defiant, carnal leader. So we're not addressing a problem limited to people in the days of Solomon. Defiance, like taxes, will forever be with us.

HOW GOD REACTED

Let's see what God did in response to Solomon's defiance. His very first reaction was *a strong statement of divine anger.*

> Now the Lord was angry with Solomon because his heart was turned away from the Lord, the God of Israel, who had appeared to him twice, and had commanded him concerning this thing, that he should not go after other gods; but he did not observe what the Lord had commanded. So the Lord said to Solomon, "Because you have done this, and you have not kept My covenant and My

statutes, which I have commanded you, I
will surely tear the kingdom from you,
and will give it to your servant."
(vv. 9–11)

Right off the bat: *"Now the Lord was angry
with Solomon."* What a refreshing balance!
What a clean breath of air! Of course God
was angry! Week after week we hear of the
love of God. We are told of the compassion
and the mercy and the grace of God, and we
surely should be. But to the exclusion of His
anger? I think not. How easy to forget that
He is holy. How seldom we hear teaching of
the wrath and the anger of God, of the jeal-
ousy God has for the purity of His people.

Mark it down in bold print: **Defiance
still makes God mad.**

A while back, I did a scriptural study on
divine anger. To tell you the truth, I was
amazed at how often the word *anger* appears
in the Bible in relation to God. Usually, the
word *kindled* accompanies the phrase. His
anger is often kindled. Our English word has
in mind the idea of arousing or stirring
something up or starting embers to glow. It's
usually related to the kindling of a fire. The
Hebrew word translated *kindled* comes from
the root verb that suggests "to be heated to
the point of vexation." It vexes God when
He sees His children walk against His plan. I
repeat, it still makes Him mad.

I have several old Puritan books. Every

time I read them, I find myself reminded of the holiness of God. God stands ready to deal with His people, modern-day teaching notwithstanding. We need the reminder that He is still jealous for our hearts, and when we walk against His way, He deals with us. The Bible is replete with illustrations such as these. Patient? Yes. Loving? Of course. Merciful? Always. But holy? And jealous? Absolutely. Never, ever forget that when we serve the idols of our own lives, the Lord becomes angry because our hearts are turned off to Him. Even His longsuffering has a limit; His patience reaches an end.

It's like what my folks used to say when I finally went too far. In a tone clearly reserved for finality, they would say: "Charles, that's it!" Oh—those awful two words! "That's it!" How I would long for a place to hide . . . or the coming of the Lord for His own! At times God says to His children, "That's it! No more!" And He moves right in. Defiance, I find more often than any other attitude, is the thing that kindles God's anger. Let us never forget that our defiance gives Him every right to be angry. We've broken His holy plan for us. He wants us to walk in the light, in fellowship with Him, just as He is in the light.

Did you notice how God said He would remove Solomon's kingdom? According to verse 11, He would "*tear*" the kingdom from him. T-E-A-R. When we exhibit defiance, forcing the Lord to step in and deal with us, it is a *tearing* experience. It's a ripping away of things that are very, very important to us. Our peace and calm are disturbed. Our diplomatic relationships with people are stirred up. We don't get along with our parents. We don't get along with our kids. We don't get along with our peers as we once did. All of that is a tearing away of kingdoms that were built in defiance.

Let's not overlook the Lord's mercy here. He says in verses 12 and 13:

> Nevertheless I will not do it in your days for the sake of your father David, but I will tear it out of the hand of your son. However, I will not tear away all the kingdom, but I will give one tribe to your son for the sake of My servant David and for the sake of Jerusalem which I have chosen.

Those are hard, strong words. Defiant people only hear hard, strong words. They are not listening to the whisperings or the quiet movements of God.

OK, what else does the Lord do? After stating His anger, *He raises up human adversaries.* Look at how He does this—it's very intriguing. Get a pencil handy and look at verse 14 and then verse 23.

> Then the Lord raised up an adversary to Solomon, Hadad the Edomite; he was of the royal line in Edom. (v. 14)

> God also raised up another adversary to him, Rezon the son of Eliada, who had fled from his lord Hadadezer king of Zobah. (v. 23)

Take a moment and underscore two identical phrases. Verse 14: *"The Lord raised up an adversary to Solomon."* Verse 23: *"God also raised up another adversary to him."* The Lord names both adversaries: Hadad and Rezon.

Why would I make a point out of these ancient, unknown names? Well, trust me . . . there is a very practical reason. Hadad and Rezon were two men who had become enemies of David. Perhaps Solomon didn't even know that fact, since he had been a little boy during most of the years of his father's life on the battlefield. He wasn't even born when his father began to clear the deck and clean house, making ready for a new kingdom . . . but Hadad never forgot it.

Look again at verse 14:

> Then the Lord raised up an adversary to Solomon, Hadad the Edomite; he was of the royal line in Edom.

So Hadad was a prince on his way to becoming a king in Edom. The verses that follow fill in all the historical details:

> For it came about, when David was in Edom, and Joab the commander of the army had gone up to bury the slain, and had struck down every male in Edom (for Joab and all Israel stayed there six

months, until he had cut off every male in Edom), that Hadad fled to Egypt, he and certain Edomites of his father's servants with him, while Hadad was a young boy. And they arose from Midian and came to Paran; and they took men with them from Paran and came to Egypt, to Pharaoh king of Egypt, who gave him a house and assigned him food and gave him land. (vv. 15–18)

Years earlier, when David took the throne, the Edomites were wiped out. Under David's direction, the Israelites slaughtered every Edomite male except a few that escaped, one of whom was Hadad of the royal line in Edom. He fled to Egypt as a little boy along with a few of the servants—no one else got out alive. Hadad remembered, from those frightening early years, the incredible slaughter that had accompanied the reign of David. And he never forgot it.

Hadad went to Egypt. He grew up there. In fact, it says in the next two verses:

Now Hadad found great favor before Pharaoh, so that he gave him in marriage the sister of his own wife, the sister of Tahpenes the queen. And the sister of Tahpenes bore his son Genubath, whom Tahpenes weaned in Pharaoh's house; and Genubath was in Pharaoh's house among the sons of Pharaoh. (vv. 19–20)

Hadad had married the sister-in-law of the Pharaoh of Egypt. He became quite a man in

Egypt. They had a son, and their son played together with the Pharaoh's kids in the Egyptian palace. Hadad was very close to the top man in Egypt . . . and he never forgot David, never.

I think Solomon probably knew nothing of Hadad. He was an Edomite, a former king-in-the-making who never made it. He was a forgotten man. But not to God. You see, when the Lord saw the defiance in Solomon's life, He began to whistle for the adversaries, much like you would call the dogs on an attacker. "Hadad, sic him!"

All of a sudden, Hadad got word that David was dead.

> But when Hadad heard in Egypt that David slept with his fathers, and that Joab the commander of the army was dead, Hadad said to Pharaoh, "Send me away, that I may go to my own country." Then Pharaoh said to him, "But what have you lacked with me, that behold, you are seeking to go to your own country? And he answered, "Nothing; nevertheless you must surely let me go." (vv. 21–22)

The writer of this narrative doesn't tell us everything here—just remember Hadad. The way this writer chronicles the story is rather intriguing. He keeps us wondering and waiting. There's another adversary the Lord used to afflict Solomon.

> God also raised up another adversary to
> him, Rezon the son of Eliada, who had
> fled from his lord Hadadezer king of
> Zobah. And he gathered men to himself
> and became leader of a marauding band,
> after David slew them of Zobah; and
> they went to Damascus and stayed there,
> and reigned in Damascus. (vv. 23–24)

The Hebrew says that Rezon led "men who
killed." The marauding band was a killing
body of men. Rezon is living in Damascus,
and Solomon doesn't know anything about
him. Everything is going well with extrava-
gant Solomon. He's waltzing along the first
twenty years of his life, relaxing. All kinds of
palaces, storehouses, and cities are being
built. And everything is working perfectly.
But erosion is happening. Ever so silently
Solomon turns against God, knowing nothing about a guy named Hadad or another
one named Rezon. Neither of them, how-
ever, will ever forget David and his reign.
Finally, both men make their long-awaited
move. Operation revenge!

> So [Rezon] was an adversary to Israel all
> the days of Solomon, along with the evil
> that Hadad did; and he abhorred Israel
> and reigned over Aram. (v. 25)

So there was evil done against Solomon
by Hadad. There was also havoc wrought by
another adversary named Rezon. I take it
that from this time on, these guys began to
harass and make life generally miserable for

a king who hadn't even known the bad dogs existed. God unleashed both of them: "Sic 'em, Hadad! Sic 'em, Rezon!"

Talk about practicality! When we have the audacity to defy the living God, when we walk against His holiness and resist His authority over our lives, He has ways of calling all kinds of dogs from any number of alleys. We don't even know they are there, then boom! He brings them in. Sometimes they come in the form of a memory ... it haunts you, it won't leave you alone. And it stays there and plagues you. It stays on top of you. You find yourself restless. It's like a monkey on your back—it stays, plagues, works, harasses, beats you black and blue emotionally. Perhaps your sense of defiance gets stronger, and you stiffen your neck and stand your ground. Guess what? God just calls more of those dogs out of the alley. "Go get him. Work on him." Need I remind you? God never runs low on dogs. He is persistent when dealing with defiance. He will not give relief to His children who deliberately walk away from His will. That includes your children who may have grown up in the Lord but are now running wild. They have their own Rezons and Hadads, trust me. It's just a matter of time before they will surrender.

I memorized a statement by Lord Byron many years ago. I find the content appropriate and penetrating: "The thorns which I have reap'd are of the tree / I planted; they have torn me, and I bleed./ I should have known what fruit would spring from such a seed."[3] Seeds that one plants grow. Often they bear ugly, treacherous thorns. They grow to such proportions that they bite and sting and hurt and infect us. God uses those thorns to prick us, to bring us back in line. Why? He's jealous for our lives. He misses the close relationship He once had with us.

There is one more person you should meet. Solomon's other two adversaries brought external oppression. This man brought internal rebellion. Those others lived outside the country—one in Egypt and one in Damascus. Their attacks and skirmishes were from the outside. Not Jeroboam. He was a man whom Solomon trusted.

> Then Jeroboam the son of Nebat, an Ephraimite of Zeredah, Solomon's servant, whose mother's name was Zeruah, a widow, also rebelled against the king.... Now the man Jeroboam was a valiant warrior, and when Solomon saw that the young man was industrious, he appointed him over all the forced labor of the house of Joseph. (vv. 26–28)

And Jeroboam went right on up the ladder. He had all the "moxie," so Solomon promoted him.

The insightful British pastor Alexander Whyte, in his biography on Old Testament characters, gives us a thumbnail sketch of Jeroboam: "It was amid all the terrible oppression and suffering of that day that Jeroboam rose so fast and so high in Solomon's service. Jeroboam's outstanding talents in public affairs, his skillful management of men, his great industry, and his great loyalty, as was thought, all combined to bring the son of Nebat under Solomon's royal eye, till there was no trust too important, and no promotion too high for young Jeroboam."[4] Then to crown it all, as time went on, he became the king's personal confidant.

Wow, that's Jeroboam—on his way to the top of the kingdom ladder. Why? He had won the heart of the king. And smack-dab in the middle of this promotion, wham! He turned and rebelled against Solomon. Did you catch that in verse 26? *"[He] rebelled against the king."*

The word *rebelled* comes from a root verb in Hebrew that means "to lift one's hand against." Perhaps he physically fought with Solomon in addition to the misery that he brought the king. What an adversary! He did an "inside job" on Solomon.

So Solomon, who months before had known only relaxation and extravagance to the point of boredom, is now faced with bulldogs like Hadad and Rezon, as well as a sleek Doberman, Jeroboam, biting and snarling and fighting with him—the king.

There is a proverb that aptly describes Solomon's woe. *"The way of the treacherous is hard"* (Prov. 13:15b). You can't defy the living Lord without having misery move in alongside.

David writes in Psalm 32:

> For day and night Thy hand was heavy upon me;
>
> My vitality was drained away as with the fever heat of summer. (v. 4)

The Lord's hounds are a lot more effective than the FBI's finest. He *always* gets His man—or woman—always! He knows where we are all the time. He won't give up.

Living in a tough situation at home right now? Having difficulty with defiance among those who work under you or over you? The Lord has never met His match. He is never intimidated by defiance. He just moves so slowly sometimes, doesn't He? Don't you wish He'd get on His horse and ride faster? "Come on, Lord, how long is this gonna take?" I understand. I've asked the same question.

Verse 40 of 1 Kings 11 says,

> Solomon sought therefore to put Jeroboam to death; but Jeroboam arose and fled to Egypt to Shishak king of Egypt, and he was in Egypt until the death of Solomon.

As if the presence of adversaries weren't bad enough, he also encounters *personal frustra-*

tion. I mean, here's the king. Surely he ought to be able to kill anybody in the land. He's even got an army available. But here's a guy who escapes! Solomon is so frustrated—he can't even put a hit man on Jeroboam and finish him off. It's as if his hands are tied. So it is when you're in defiance; things refuse to work out. Try all you like, you cannot find relief in wrongdoing.

THE DOWNWARD SPIRAL
OF DEFIANCE

Talk about going from bad to worse. Defiance is the classic illustration. First, *defiance begins with carnal attitudes.* Long before there are carnal actions, there are carnal attitudes. It can happen to adults just as quickly as it can to teens or kids. Perhaps it would help if I spelled out a few of the attitudes by describing some actual thoughts in the minds of the defiant. The first thought says, "I want my own way." Those who are defiant aren't interested in your way, or God's way. "I want *my* way." That is an attitude of *selfishness.*

The second thought says this: "I won't quit until I get it." That is an attitude of *stubbornness.* "I want my way, and I want it when I want it. And I will not quit until I get it." That's just plain obstinance; that's stubbornness.

Third: "I don't care who it hurts." In other words, "I want my way. I won't quit until I get it, and I don't care who it hurts—husband, wife, peers, kids, the team, my church—I don't care. I'm gonna get my way." That is an attitude of *indifference*.

Fourth: "I refuse to listen to counsel." Obviously, that is an attitude of *resistance*. "I know He has something to tell me, but I don't want to hear what He's got to say." Or, "I know what He's going to tell me. I know what that book says. I don't want to listen to God's counsel." That's resistance.

Fifth, and finally: "I am not concerned about the consequences." That's *contempt*. Pushed to the wall, this extreme reaction includes ignoring the consequences—a total lack of concern for the results.

"I want my own way. I won't quit until I get it. I don't care who it hurts. I will not listen to counsel. I am not concerned about the consequences." Those are the words of a defiant person. And they can come from our lips just as readily as from a person without Christ. They represent selfishness and stubbornness and indifference and resistance and contempt. As I mentioned earlier, defiance begins with carnal attitudes.

Continuing the downward spiral, the second inescapable reality about defiance is this: *Defiance leads to personal misery.* Remember Hadad, Rezon, and Jeroboam? They dealt Solomon untold misery. The defiant person wants freedom, but he finds himself captured. He wants his own way, but he finds himself ensnared by the restrictions that misery brings.

Look at Proverbs 13:15 and you'll see a pretty good illustration or statement of that kind of misery. I referred to it earlier but now want to examine two particular terms:

> Good understanding produces favor,
> But the way of the treacherous is
> hard.

The word *treacherous* is translated from the Hebrew verb that means "to deal treacherously or defiantly." The way of one who deals in defiance is *hard*. Interesting term. It means "to be perpetual, steady, constant, ever enduring, rugged." The etymology of the term finally leads to ruggedness. The way of the person who deals in defiant thoughts and actions is perpetually rugged, hard, and miserable. Not only Solomon's life but a proverb from Scripture assures us that defiance leads to personal misery.

There is a third stage on this downward spiral: *Defiance results in inescapable bondage.* Those most defiant are most bound, not free.

> For the ways of a man are before the
> eyes of the Lord,
> And He watches all his paths. (Prov.
> 5:21)

That is quite a thought. But the next two verses complete the picture:

His own iniquities will capture the
wicked,
And he will be held with the cords of
his sin.
He will die for lack of instruction,
And in the greatness of his folly he
will go astray.

Look at that! The "*cords*" from one's own
defiance will wrap themselves around the
victim and will cause him to be inescapably
bound up. In the margin of my mind I have
written "Samson," who was literally bound
with the cords of his own sin—unconquered
lust.

Frankly, I'm much more concerned
about "acceptable" defiance than *bold* defiance. Why? Because that is what happens
more often than not. We cover up. We hide
our defiance. We sit on the lid. But, sure
enough—given sufficient pressure—something snaps.

Leonard Held was a paragon of
respectability. He was a middle-aged, hard-
working lab technician who had worked at
the same Pennsylvania paper mill for nine-
teen years. Having been a Boy Scout leader,
an affectionate father, a member of the local
fire brigade, and a regular churchgoer, he
was admired as a model in his community,
until ... his image exploded in a well-
planned hour of bloodshed one brisk Octo-
ber morning. Held decided to mount a

one-man revolt against the world he inwardly resented.

A proficient marksman, he stuffed two pistols into his coat pockets—a .45 automatic, and a Smith and Wesson .38. He drove his station wagon to the mill and parked quietly. Gripping a gun in each fist, he then slowly stalked into the shop. He started shooting with such calculated frenzy that it resembled a scene out of the old TV program "Gunsmoke." He filled several of his fellow workmen with two or three bullets apiece, firing more than thirty shots in all. He deliberately killed some of the men he had known for over fifteen years.

When a posse was formed to capture the man, they found him standing in his doorway, snarling defiantly, "Come and get me. I'm not taking any more of your bull." Total bewilderment swept over the neighborhood. Puzzled policemen and friends finally discovered a tenuous chain of reasoning behind his brief reign of terror. I believe deep within the heart and soul of Leonard Held rumbled the giants of defiance and resentment. The man who had appeared like a monk on the outside was seething with hatred, treacherous defiance within.

Several of Held's victims had been promoted over him, while he remained in the same position at the shop. More than one in his car pool had quit riding with him due to his reckless driving. A neighbor had been threatened and struck by him after an argument over a fallen tree. Held was brimming with resentful rage that could not be restrained any longer.

The caption near his picture in *Time* magazine told the truth: "Responsible, respectable—and resentful."[5] Leonard Held was a man of defiance.

Your defiance will come out in the most amazing ways—a battered child; a crime of passion; a blistering tongue-lashing; running away from home; an illicit pregnancy; an ugly, caustic line of profane words; an affair; domestic disharmony; a ruined testimony. I charge you before God to deal severely with this giant. It may be slumbering right now— but I warn you—not for long.

Now that you have reached the end of this booklet, I would like you to think about your life for just a few moments. I'd like you to trace your actions and attitudes back a day or two, or maybe several weeks. Take a long, straightforward look at where you are. Are any signs of defiance there? "I want my own way. I won't quit till I get it. I don't care who it hurts. I refuse to listen to counsel. I'm not concerned about consequences."

Now, my friend, those are dangerous words. If they are there in your head, you're on a powder keg that's going to explode. I ask you to find the hope of forgiveness in

Jesus Christ. He is there, and He awaits your turning all that turmoil over to Him . . . that hot caldron of resentment. The longer it boils the more lethal could be the result.

If you've never met Jesus Christ personally, He's the one to whom you turn first. He died for that sin and all your other sins, too. Don't rationalize and say, "Well, that's just the way I am." Call it what it is and say, "Lord, I come to You in my need. I need You to take it; take it now."

I ask, heavenly Father, that in a very personal and wonderful way You will bring cleansing and hope. Some who read this booklet are Your children. Some are not. I pray for both groups. Defiance is such an aggressive enemy! Replace our selfishness, our stubbornness, our indifference, our resistance, our contempt . . . with *forgiveness*. Release us from the bondage of our sin, dear God.

I invite You to take a walk down the galleries of our minds and lift those pictures off the wall that have no business being there. And flood us with Your forgiveness, Father. Take away all the sting from the long-standing thorns that we're living with. Do this now, Father. In the name of Jesus I pray. Amen.

[1] The Living Bible (Wheaton, Ill.: Tyndale House Publishers, 1971).

[2] *The Holy Bible: The Berkeley Version in Modern English* (Grand Rapids: Zondervan Publishing House, 1959).

[3] Lord George Noel Gordon Byron, "Childe Harold's Pilgrimage," canto 4, stanza 10, in *Familiar Quotations*, ed. John Bartlett (Boston: Little, Brown & Co., 1955), 453–54.

[4] Alexander Whyte, *Bible Characters: The Old Testament* (London: Oliphants Ltd.; Grand Rapids: Zondervan Publishing House, 1952), 382.

[5] "The Revolt of Leo Held," *Time*, 90 (November 3, 1967), 21–22.

Other Booklets by Chuck Swindoll:

Anger

Attitudes

Commitment

Demonism

Destiny

Divorce

Eternal Security

Fun is Contagious

God's Will

Hope

Impossibilities

Integrity

Leisure

The Lonely Whine of the Top Dog

Moral Purity

Our Mediator

Peace ... in Spite of Panic

The Power of a Promise

Prayer

Sensuality

Singleness

Stress

This is No Time for Wimps!

Tongues

When Your Comfort Zone Gets the Squeeze

Woman